My Dreaming Waking Life

Six Poets Sixty-Six Poems

Elaine Starkman
Joseph Chaiklin
Florence Miller
Dave Holt
S. Solomon
Marc Hofstadter

The six Northern California poets who contributed to this book meet monthly to read and critique each other's work.

Art and Cover Design by Bruce Estes

First published by Dog Ear Publishing
4010 W. 86th Street, Ste H
Indianapolis, IN 46268
www.dogearpublishing.net

ISBN: 978-159858-965-8
Library of Congress Control Number: 2009931902

This book is printed on acid-free paper.

Printed in the United States of America

Contents

Elaine Starkman

Joseph Chaiklin

Florence Miller

Dave Holt

S. Solomon

Marc Hofstadter

Elaine Starkman

My Dreaming Waking Life

I ride a plum pony
between my knees

lovely little one
just for me

Into my old flat
we prance

behind our old store
too small for ponies

Orchid pony and I
Round and round

Lavender
splashing sky

Mama says
Get it out of here

Daddy says
Keep him

Thus I begin my
Dreaming waking life

For Six Days

It rains sadness
I talk to few

I write a poem
I tear it up

On the seventh day
The Sun God Ra

Flings arcs of rainbow
Throughout the sky

O lark ascending
O bluebird over

My death
My very life

Photo of a Couple at Pt. Lobos

You stand there in our son's jacket
white stubble on your chin

snapping shots with the camera I bought
for your birthday then took for my own

In the nip of air you pose me
against a rock

Sea lions yelp   seagulls flap
and you who are so calm

shout above the sounds:
    Look, a whale!

And I who have waited all winter
to spot that dark hump on the horizon

say nothing as if I were you   as if
my eyes were wet from seablow

Yet at the same instant
think myself grey bent

first you gone then I too
late twentieth century photo

snapped shut in an album
that distant relatives browse

like tourists in a museum

Apricots for Isaac

The sky was a clear jewel
my grandson and I roamed
an open orchard, one of the last,

a space between the park
and my house. He was a spy walking
the bumpy path, not the sidewalk.

He had just begun to worry about foxtails
sticking in his socks when he saw apricot trees
hung with fruit, not yet golden nor ripe,

but small globes of gold and orange,
He gave me his spy cap and climbed up.
"Here, Grandma," he called,

throwing them down to me
with a child's delight I'd forgotten,
21st century Tom Sawyer, with red hair and freckles.

In the abandoned orchard
picking apricots and chasing off ants,
I remembered lost worlds:

I hadn't seen fruit-bearing trees
until my twenties and by thirty,
had no time to savor them.

Only now do I know
what I'd mistaken for wisdom.

Northern California Freeway, 8:30 a.m.

With his enormous antlers he rams into my
car door wildly eyeing me as I wait
to move. I'm frightened, but I let him in.

People swear in seven different tongues:
Bitch, you could have killed us! Fucking Prius!

I've never had an animal
this large in a car, just children's pets.
He speaks to me in sounds,
grunts and whines; his soft brown eyes
roll in his head.

A buck hit along 680 at 8 a.m.
What will I do with him, his bleeding,
stench, waning breath, stiffening coat.
Where can I take him as all the car radios blare:

> *40,000 in Pakistan Sunnis and Shiites*
> *floods hurricanes earthquakes*
> *rising poverty global warming*

But at this moment I don't care
about them, only this deer.

West Coast East Coast

You know this to be true: flying 35,000 feet above earth
in April with ice on your window real miles exist between coasts,
3,000 of them. Real space, time and distance, mere pretense

in air: my watch says eight but it's eleven plus the possibility
the plane could dive down so that Nicholson and Keaton
are mere film where you live out your cravings.

In reverse, images in an East Coast magazine offer small truths.
You return to a self that dictates directions of your life.
Then on the subway a man acts out.

You dream you shout "Stop!"—you who don't know
your way from 42nd Street to 86th, who resist maps and hope
magic carries you on your journey.

What if the man hears you as if you were an essay
you'll read on women and power at Poets House
on Spring Street? Borders blur between wakefulness

and dream while small groups of subway toughs
are turned around by your thoughts, by sudden
nutriment of Hassidic songs. Psalms stud the air.

Petitions pass from Spanish speakers on trains
through the halls of St. Paul's and St. Andrew's
to the Argentine rabbi, psalms gallop across pampas

into your ears: you and the rest of America
must pray for peace this week of bombings.
On a second train packed with hordes rides.

one man who is different in his 50's black coat,
collarless white shirt, Kafka-like except
with blue translucent eyes. He hovers

over his seat, he's here and not here—like you
Where's he going? Perhaps he has no destination.
Perhaps he has reached it—this ice on your
plane's window. Is this prequel or sequel?

Late Eulogy for Joseph Brodsky
U.S. Poet Laureate, 1991-1992

Not many gather this spring day   a few old Russians,
stocky, broad-boned cousins from a distant past and young ones
mod as Calvin Klein. Sprinklings of gray-haired Americans—

small audience for a man expelled from his birthplace
who carried two typewriters one with Cyrillic
one with Latin letters and nothing more than

his eloquence, his green ink pens, grief and reason.
He lived in two languages. A sad mouth scowls from
his photo, this poet who died young in America—

one who knew the burn of fire against his face.
He writes so humbly of aged parents that I dream
of my own failing mother and dead father:
> *unbearable laughter thirteen square meters*
> *bread on the table, a synonym for life,*
> *visits denied until: Mama is no more, you know.*

Across vast space of jumbled cables, wires,
and endless calls between countries, he writes:
> *death is a passage outward*
> *into the domain of a telescope or prayer...*
> *I write this in English so that it may live...*
> *I return like an echo...here there can be no memory...*

San Francisco, 1992/2006

Going to Siberia
for Dr. M

I lead you follow
in bitter white wind

I'm at home here,
its past is mine not yours—

you don't know a thing
among slabs of ice

frozen old stoves   gulags   murderers
more than half century ago

Here I know how to move
you freeze for all your theories

I move past my self
and sex   old soul

who's lived here before—
work camps   death camps

prisons that promise nothing
I know this blinding light

I leap and jump
dragging you with me

We drink cups of kvass
exit this glare where everything's dead

At my command the dogs drag
us along frostbit fingers entwined

Oh Siberia Siberia
in your depths

I find you
in my dual nature

Second Viewing: Four Women Impressionists
Legion of Honor, San Francisco, July 2008

Through the crowds of gay pride, up Geary to view four women's art,
one American, three French (one by way of Spain through family).
Don't rush, stop, linger, learn: all are different. Not a sisterhood, but
all restricted to paint in home and garden. Begin slowly: **Mary Cassatt**,
American friend of Degas: stubborn, unmarried, childless. A woman
bathes a child, perhaps against epidemics of 19th century cholera;

another Cassatt—the haunting sadness of "The Mandolin Player,"
atypical, strong lines. Yet muted. Let crowds hurry by. You'll return
to her. She says, *Women should be someone, not something.*
Slowly, slowly you must move on to **Eva Gonzales** dead at 34,
three weeks after childbirth, her paintings of women so shaded
I feel they seem to move. In her short life she paints a woman in white,

a sleeping woman, a waking woman, soft smile on her lips, perhaps
after sex. Now carried with rushed crowd, move to **Marie Bracquemond**
who stops painting when her print-maker husband scolds
she has no talent. Here Monsieur judges Madame across the dinner
table; she looks away. Born into sadness, she dies a recluse.
Sadly, slowly, back to Cassatt, later in life, blinded by cataracts.

Is it possible to *paint not flowers but feelings*? They ask,
and ask again *Does marriage end art? Can women paint
as well as men? Is their space dug deep into a two-D canvas?*

Women pulling on stockings, reading, walking in the rain.
Cassatt has been so reproduced that I dismiss her for the
lesser known. Cassatt snaps:

Wait!
Pay attention to my life!
Don't mull over yourself!

Ah. Yet one more whose work I know. Time is short, the rooms fill.
Berthe Morisot paints in *plein air* filled with spring light and lush
wild shimmering movement; she marries Manet's brother, now paints

their daughter Julie indoors, friend to Renoir who still thinks women
artists ridiculous, though Morisot, a rare woman, shows her work in Paris.
By now the rooms bend, blend artists' differences and likenesses,

one implores, *reclaim pastels;* one shades a woman's cheek blue,
one is aggrieved with silence—and my pen too is silent—

"31 Flavors Invade Japan/French Vanilla"
on a painting by Masami Teraoka—

Her face floats restrained, real, surreal
reborn in 1979 ancient, alive.
She's frightened and frightening
plucking a koto—
Ping, ping, pong sounds fly into the *Japan Times*
where across the ocean a gay boy
plucks another ancient instrument
and is killed for it in California.

In another language but with same flashing colors
there's a stoplight near a disco.
Napkins shooting out of dispensers
for her French Vanilla cone.

Her hair is pulled so tightly it gives her
a headache; she cannot think only act.
(there's yen in it for a comfort woman)
In ribbons and curlers she has utmost reserve
plus reverence for the baths, American slang,
and hatred for all emperors without clothes.

In high priced love hotels she rules them,
those round-eyed foreigners, who flash
their false smiles at heated toilet seats
at the same time gagging
on MacDonald's burgers
                                and raw fish.

Come Back Alice
for Aura Edwards

1
Bring back my blue
Caterpillar whole
True Cheshire cats
With real smiles
Packs of cards with honest dealers
Tumbling not inside the earth
But landing on their feet
Let every un-birthday burst through
A land of wonder

2
Come back anew Alice
End execution without trial
Tainted torts and tarts
Rotted cabbages and rotten kings
I'll keep brillig and my whimsy
Hold my tea tray in the sky
But tear off my child apron
Fit me to my true size

3
Come back Alice
Let me be all that I can
Let running rabbits
Who are always late
Finally find the exact date
Let hatters fit a healthy hat
Let eggs exist for all to eat
Fit me to my true size

4

Come back true self
Let the earth keep moving
Help me find
What I'm pursuing
Where's my list
I'm not abiding
How can I know
What is so
Fit me to my true size

Joseph Chaiklin

Felicia

Felicia, phantom of my fourth grade year,
was a silent, sad presence in our class
who once maybe twice a week appeared
among us wrapped always all day in
a long brown wool coat that let us see
only her alabaster face and hands.
We didn't speak to her or she to us;
perhaps we didn't know the words to say.
But what did we know about why she was
so seldom with us during that fleeting year?
We didn't know what I surely know now—
that the coat she clutched about her on
all those hot, warm or cold days was
holding life in as it held death out.

Oh Felicia, if the me of me now could
be there with the you of you then,
I'd take my still familiar place beside you,
look into your pale blue eyes and say
"Good morning Felicia; how are you today?
I've missed you forever."

Meat

What will it be for dinner tonight?
If it is beef, broil blood rare,
serve seasoned well with guilt.
If shark, grill to moist perfection,
serve with well-deserved remorse.
If veal, bread and fry golden brown,
serve with pain inflicted without mercy.
Serve no wine with these meals,
just a draft of tears with love distilled.
For dessert, let there be honey-glazed
bits of bone from dwindling creatures.

Her Diary
for Fronie

In the final weeks, during the duel
between her pain and her painkillers,
in an unsteady hand she wrote each day
in a diary things like: who was expected
the next day, at what time, who stayed
too long, what pleased her, or not, an
illustrated plan to rearrange the furniture
in her room, and how an uninvited chaplain
suggested Bible passages to soothe her.
He told some nice stories, she noted.
Her diary was a slim chronicle of how
she controlled the countdown of her
remaining days. An entry near the end
summarized her philosophy of love
so concisely it might make philosophers
blush. It read, *Love is an all out affair*
at the center of all people and things.
The day before the coma she wrote that
she hoped *to go home via one of hospice's*
happenings, that her coolness continued,
how she loved it and the breeze that
came with it and that she hoped
to feel the coolness that night.

Wireless

Everywhere is where they are,
where with graceless disregard
they talk and talk without end
into the sleek killers of quiet
contemplation connected to
their ears one way or the other.
Silence seems to them an absent
consideration as they inflict on all
about them private complaints,
discontents and trivialities.
What do I wish for these noisy
magpies and kuckaburras who
so disturb our thoughts?
I wish them swift flight to
a tranquil distant forest where
wood nymphs may teach
them to be like the snake
silent and seldom seen.

An Ugly Business

When I was thirty-five I placed an airline
poster on my office wall, a bullfighting scene
that beckoned me to Spain to a contest
about which I knew barely more than nothing.
Damn, that picture was beautiful!
Its matador postured gracefully—fearless and
imperious, in a sequined costume of turquoise,
gold and black, furling a purple and yellow
cape above his head as the charging bull missed.
I don't know how long the picture pleased me,
but only long enough for me to understand
that bullfighting is an ugly business in which
a bull is taunted, pierced with colorful
barbed sticks, speared in the neck, the better
to weaken him, taunted further to exhaustion,
readied for the matador to drive from above
a sword between his tortured bleeding shoulders.
I discarded the picture when it finally breached
the boundary between humanity and love of art.

Autumn Squirrels

Autumn squirrels are busy creatures,
too busy to doubt the mutability
of acorns or the durability of oaks:
that you eat one and climb the other
is clear in a squirrel's scheme of things.
Pursuit of the necessary is also clear
in their tail-ticking search for a perfect
place to bury the nut of the moment.

When these almond-eyed searchers,
devout followers of the Book of Seasons,
pass through winter to their springtime
duties, will they pause to notice
the snow-piercing birth of the crocus?

Disorder

At the center and fringes of my life
I yearn for order in the spaces where
I live, order defined in simple things—
the kitchen counter laid bare of
objects strewn in careless disarray,
bare to the granite's simple beauty;
the dining room table decluttered
to the essence of its pleasing grain;
the lamp table by my chair holding
nothing but what is needed now.
I crave order in these things even
as I subvert it by careless intent.
Gods of clutter and disarray, deliver me
from the chaos of my disordered way.

How My Father Became Dead

Dead is what my father is,
but I can't tell you that he died,
for that does not begin to say what
caused him to become dead
on a clear Sunday morning
in November forty years ago.

He entered the crosswalk more
sure than you or I that green
would grant him passage
to the opposite curb, more sure
because he had the cautious
certainty of those who live with
one eye blind, who always look
first to the light, then left, right,
and left again before they cross.

But caution was not enough
that day to save my father
from the death car speeding
through the crosswalk faster than
the last left turn of his head,
freeway fast, straight at him,
a battering ram that sent him
flying deathward, then sped
still faster to false freedom.

My voice still resists telling you
that my long-dead father died,
resists because *murdered* is
the word to tell what happened
to him on that November day, and
murdered is a word so strong
it sucks the life from *died.*

I Was Tom Wingfield

I didn't know that I was Tom Wingfield,
or who he was, until I wandered into
a brief collegiate acting career during which
I inhabited him on-stage and became Laura's
protective brother and Amanda's rebellious son.
Laura, shy, lame, more fragile than the tiny
animals in her glass menagerie, a sparkling
refuge from her life's painful center;
Amanda, abandoned wife, controlling
and out-of-control mother who lived her life
through others, but mostly through her children.

My off-stage Tom didn't have a Laura, but he was
Tom, all right, complete with his own Amanda,
a mother he loved as long as he didn't share time
and space with her. The two Toms, Tennessee's
and mine, shared more than their Amandas.
They both wrote poems that won prizes, even
fancied themselves poets, but most urgently,
shared a need to escape their relentless Amandas.
Tennessee's Tom escaped to the sea in the
Maritime Service, and mine escaped to Parris Island
where, with concealed affection, his crisp
Marine Corps drill instructor subjected him
loudly to indignities that my Tom endured
successfully because he felt that he was free.

West Nile

Where have you been my beautiful
bird-bath bullies, spring to spring,
winter to winter this year past?
I've missed you pretty ones, despite
your raucous blue jay ways, and I've
missed your brash black cousins,
the crows, with their Caw! Caw! Caws!
Did the virus claim you as it claimed
squadrons of your friends before?
Was it here mosquitoes drew your
blood and passed the virus on?
Or did you fly to a far dry place where
no mosquitoes fly sanguine missions,
where there is no death by Nile?

The Kiss

It happened in an office,
not one kiss among many
as in an office romance.
Not like that at all, just
one kiss at noon when
others were at lunch
and we were alone.
We stood talking
of things other than us,
drew close and kissed—
softly, tenderly, long.
It was thrilling, startling,
ended wordlessly as it began
and never happened again.
She was black,
I was white,
It was 1958.

Florence Miller

Raven Reads the Fog

Moving
      Always moving
The fog

Now moonstone peaks reveal themselves
 The whale-shaped snow whiter than cloud
    On Thunder Mountain
The fish-shaped rock
      The bird-shaped land
        Between the clouds
A sign

Redberry
 Mountain ash
  Sumac and alder
 Cormorants skim water
 Terns crosstitch air

Raven reads the fog
 Knows what it means when fog envelops land
    Reads leaves of trees
Tree stumps scoured by glaciers
     Slant of snowfall
 Shapes of stars
The great wing
     Folded back on itself

Salmon son of Raven out of Fog Woman
    Salmon thick in mouths of rivers
      Salmon fungus-marked for death
     And on the shore the stumps of ancient trees
            Raven waiting

Pond

for Edward Wahl

I walked to Cook's pond
With its algae and scum
Milkweed pods bursting
Goldenrod and rose hips
Past the cattails
Past the oak struck by lightning
Now red-leafed at the tip
My first fall without you
Why didn't you
Come back to our pond
Where we saw two snakes
Entwined

Still

for Donald Miller

Incense for the dead
Smoke curls
Out the window

In his ashes
Flecks of
Carnelian

Seven years
Still   the goldfish
Still impatiens

Army coat
Still the smell
Of his sweat

After Pelican Harbor

Leaving the grotto we see the fins—
Two sharks below the surface
Shadows longer than our boat

The sea a Hiroshige print
And we are in it
I swear if we get to shore
I'll never sail again

Sailing into Ventura we quarrel
I see the stacks that mark the harbor
See the clock on the gas dock
jump

Cleat the boat and hold
But the boat takes my line
Lying on the dock I scream
My finger   my finger

You make a sling with a gasoline rag
walk me to the Coast Guard
Half a block   upstairs saying
I wish it had happened to me

I say   *I wish it had*

Weather

1
The scrupulous birds
Peck at corn on the levee
Water snakes slither into holes
Thunderheads build
We scramble ashore

2
The flesh rejoices
At the shock
Of thunder
Cyclones tear the avenues
Carving the great name
On the gardens
Outside the glass conservatory

3
I thread through the wood
Wary of epitaphs
Sacred and disordered
Now I say *now*

4
A soft hum
A brew of bees
Fierce, emerging
Ready to stab as I
Jump from the ledge
Into the oak leaves

5
And is it angina
Not pain but awareness
Of death about to claim me
In this year of my joy

Forced Landing

Northern Lights pulse down the dark
Over glaciers
Over our one good engine
Over the icebergs' reach—
The captain jettisons the fuel
I watch for flames behind the wing
I am keeping the plane in the air
The old witch sings like the North Star
The sky is falling
Who will tear her pockets
And tear her hair
And beat her breast

Salvage

I numb myself
For speech what

Can we say to
Each other in

The dark I saw
Your eyes go

Dead that day I
Let the finches

Die and threw
My wedding ring

Into the bay
Yet if the house

Caught fire I'd grab
The whale-shape stone

The bone ring
You gave me

The secret screams
Connecting us

The Heart
for Edward Wahl

I saw it on the screen
Its four chambers

Heard the blood swooshing
Waterfall smashing

Cat beneath the rock's lip
Squatting in the pool

My love on a gurney
Paddles attached

Systole diastole systole
Diastole systole diastole

And later on another screen
Blood's saw-tooth code

Heart working
Almost normal

A TV weather map
The center of storm

Nothing I could ever believe
Star clusters of Andromeda

Watching at night
On the boat in the delta

Falling stars
Close enough to touch

Veil

for Donald Miller

When
You were
Transformed

Into shell
And fine sand

We scattered
You
Off Angel Island

How you lay
Like a veil
On the bay

Before
Descending

I want
To put
My mouth
In yours

Hear cold
Buds
Singing

Be warmed
By
Old suns

Ghost
for Donald Miller

I enter each room and see your ghost
I open the bag we packed for the hospital
And never used   Your flask is full of brandy
The leather marked with your sweat

I look for the face in the rock to show me a sign
But there's nothing   I feed the bird
Two fish have survived
They come to my hand when I feed them.

There is a mouse now
I saw it skittering
Behind the dresser

Flowering crab has passed full bloom
Petals seep down
The hillside

I won't live until spring   you said
I won't see you grow old

Death in Carvoeiro

Boats with eyes on prows
Search the wind for a drowned fisherman
Three days later they find him
A Belgian on vacation

A wrinkled woman weeps at the cistern
Says *I cry tears for him*
Her two dwarf sons remove their hats
In exaggerated gesture and bow

Kerosene lamps flare in fog
A boy sits on a load of wood
In his father's wagon

Death in Carvoeiro
The horse tail wound with orange wool
Cart decorated with eyes   old

We light a fire   smoke stains
the mural of fig trees
Paintings of saints

Their eyes follow us
We cannot wait for almond bloom
We leave for Lisbon in mist

Behind wagons
Before light

Dave Holt

As If We Were The First

Fogbank squatting on the beach this morning;
cloud of sadness that slowed me down,
both have fled like deer from a thicket; showing
nervous white tails, they cross Cazadero Road.

Regrets scatter like ragged fog
banished by Pacific winds—
bean plants shake off cool, fallen dew,
to stand tall, crisp in mid-morning sun.

Let us go into the garden together
to eat the fruit in season as if
we were the first man and first woman
ever to have loved like this.

Berries for breakfast,
yellow squash for supper;
come, let us go
where beanstalks climb to heaven.

To Believe as Children

To arrive in a neighborhood of tall sugar maples,
fragrance of wood smoke lingering on the air.
To clamber up lopsided steps, a country porch,
latticed verandah, rickety uneven boards
pushed willy-nilly by earth more ancient than house.
To be welcomed into a room of noise and talk,
under a brass pendant light turned up bright,
throwing shadows on faded, floral wallpaper,
brown water stained where rain leaked in.
To watch wide-eyed as gilt-edged china
lifted gently from the glass cabinet
is placed 'round a massive, oak dining room table,
grown larger with every extra leaf put in,
while the homemade bench in the garage
is fetched for the kids to share.

After endless delays, a shout from the kitchen
for all to be seated, hold hands
for the blessing. Under Grandpa's stern look
thrown to the cousins who joke and clown,
and poke each other under the white linen cloth.
There is a short embarrassed laugh from Mother,
Then we say grace, held in a circle
of light and magic.

To do all this is to believe the circle
could never disappear as children will think
being closer to something timeless,
believing important things
such as love like this
can go on forever.

Norwich, 1960

Coyote

When Aunt Lil died, Coyote told me.
That's how I discovered their relationship,
standing on the creek bank, praying for her spirit,
that was slipping into blackness.
From there, I saw Wiisagi-ma'iingan,
scramble out from under the bridge
where homeless campers hide,
limping, not from cold bones,
uneasy sleep on damp ground, but a broken foot,
held out in front, favoring the useless paw
while he rambled the last trail that was safe
for a three-legged scavenger. I knew
my aunt's spirit wandered beside him,
her own wound like Coyote's,
hopeless of healing.

She too stepped through trouble with finesse,
bluff, like Coyote with his grin and charm,
used humor, clever conversation, as a defense
from men, to submerge the rage,
girlhood memories of rape.
Attempted or real? We would never know.
She determined not to marry or have a man,
just to survive in their world, like her ally.

Trickster disappeared into tule reeds and brush,
savvy smile licked from his jaw as he turned,
goodbye grin over a shoulder, as if he shared
my Auntie's laughter, her final joke.
I never saw him in the creek bed again.

She too departed at that moment,
found her way to flower trails overhead
where Great Spirit's star-nations waited to greet her.
I didn't need my sister's call to know, to confirm.

Lillian, white lily blossom of her mother's eye,
follows the path of the Milky Way,
eager for her mother's outstretched hand
that waits to grasp her daughter's in her own,
where paws that are wounded are made whole again.

Frames of Reference

When I stopped in front of the old house,
starry-eyed for something familiar,
it neither embraced nor welcomed me as before.
Instead quiet darkness excluded this son.
Should it speak, it would claim it didn't know my name.

Across the playing field, the doomed high school,
doors and windows boarded up.
It wasn't they who let me down.
I defied them, I who was deficient,
wanting, incapable of giving.

Where is the Self? Encased in its frame?
Lost in a letterbox?
Wearing these memories
like an oversized winter coat,
fur collar flecked with snow?

I once had an insight,
my Self, a kind of tree,
parts suspended like ornaments
dangling from the branch tips
spinning in mid air like moons and planets.

It takes a self mastery—a kind of
Samkhaya Yoga—to keep it in balance—
Ego, id, soul, memory,
not as a juggler would,
not some circus act, tight rope walker,

unless I am the lion,
listening and watching
for the directing movements
of the lion tamer.

On Resisting and Embracing

The sky above recovers its blue from
a leftover storm, hangs distant billows,
suspends castle towers on eastern ramparts,
where glittering Niagara plunges
over ancient Silurian cliffs.

Viewed from her place at the center,
the long, sandy point arcs out into the lake
upon each side—two arms of land
encompass and contain her.

Hello again, she says, to renewed knowing;
sweeping her arms out   a motion
familiar from yoga   breathe deep,
      exhale slowly
           count beats
                take in light
                    and air,
embrace the beauty and heartbreak of a
log-strewn, storm-battered, Lake Erie shore.

She says goodbye to ancestors who thought
tight-lipped love should be known, understood
without being spoken, bodies stiffening
from hugs they were unable to return,
who thought this should be enough.

She wanted words, the expression,
without agonizing. Was it selfish? Wrong
for her and her brother to want that?
Her hands fly up to cover her ears,
stop this obsessive sibilance
about what they didn't do for us.

Remember instead their good gifts.

But unspoken love leaves too much room
for mischief, wickedness — plenty of it
weeding up, twining among cornstalks
that whisper to blue chicory
and wind-tossed day lilies
that gossip with Queen Anne's lace
about lies, blood-red berry vines,
black thorns of sunny youth revisited.

She fears evil in the family's secret heart,
not hers to contend with,
or resist. Her brother may argue,
demand his due, disagree
when she says,
leave it alone, Will.

She trusts Spirit to transform it,
root it out.

Homage, Facing the Four Directions

You slayed me but I rose again,
Sideswiped me but I got back on the road.
Found myself in a gutter,
Then you brought me to the tall mountain.

I'd been carting trophies home in wheelbarrows,
News-clippings, accomplishments followed by the media.
Cherishing the fickle attention of strangers,
I raked in the paltry winnings of notoriety.

You staggered me but I found my sea legs,
Rolled me and left my pockets full of changes.
Was knocked out cold,
But I woke up in a sweet dream.

What was it in the intimate atmosphere of you
To capture this breathless moon in its orbit?
Such true good earth you held in cupped hands,
Did you know you possessed such solidity?

No, you looked up in surprise at the gift,
same as I, to find open road ahead, boulders rolled away.
Howls of creatures in the wilderness, now fading,
dying away on the wind far behind us.

Tiba's Scout

I, a runner, chosen to leave at first light,
to scout a trail across the Isthmus
to the crest of the Andean Cordillera.
I'd run the road before, met hazards in low places.
One morning, I encountered Jaguar on the path.
Jaguar, a god I knew.
I sat down, relaxed, in front of him,
as if only to soak up the first rays of sun,
closed my eyes, entered into a deep concentration,
and talked to him. No words. No sound from my lips.
I told him of changes afoot, White God coming,
and Balboa, my people called Tiba, his servant,
whom I now served.

Snarls and growls died away to panting
as he circled. I listened to soft footpads,
his black mind considering, hot breath
on my arm as he sniffed with curiosity,
prickled my body hair, goosebumping skin,
then suddenly, unexpectedly, gone.
Back to his unassailable jungle.

I got up and ran, spread my arms out
to soar like Condor, chest to sky,
feeling wind blow fragrant air
through my pores into grateful lungs.
Running now towards something new,
requiring, eliciting, added strength, courage;
I no longer fled from footsteps behind me,
nor from primeval fear of Jaguar.
I was liberated. New meanings in the song
I chanted as feet flew free over hard clay:

"My self-knowing is complete; I am strong,
a vehicle for the king, I prepare the way.
Progress is certain, victory sure.
My legs carry the message,
hope for the future,
for he now comes."

The road was clear of enemies,
Fearing Tiba's sword and horse,
the natives had deserted their villages.
I reached the crest of the ridge overlooking the sea.
Tiba calls it Mar del Sur. It stretched away
without end to a misty horizon.
Hawk circled above in the pale haze,
the only living one in sight
besides a breathless, panting runner.

On the Shores of San Pablo Sea

I study the humped corpse of Round Top, looking
for the once ravenous, flame-red mouth of it,
burnt out volcano in the Berkeley Hills, keeled over
on one side, in death, or sleep; the basaltic cone,
points its crooked finger eastward. No one I know
can show the crater plain to my eyes.
All this while waiting out a light rain, huddled
under pines, watching winter showers pass overhead.

Made it to the grove in time. Dark clouds
drifted in, like warning ghosts, plaits of gray
that sweep the bay's shining surface.

Rufous-sided towhees forage in thickets,
I catch sight of the white spotted shoulders.
Even this quiet moment away from traffic,
I want wondrous things to see. Time runs short,
opportunities dwindle, as if Nature must deliver
on the same strict schedule observed by industry.
I am thinking "She" does not provide that way,
but yields up treasures, magic unbidden,
moments of beauty to patient watchers.

On this day I search perhaps with desperation
for hope and direction, having lost a good job,
been handed many days to hike mountains and canyons
hidden from the world and its commerce.
Our obsession with acquisition dissolves.

Another clue among scrub and thorn, a decorated bird,
myself as a youth, an impression: unspoiled.
Can hope be recaptured? Still baffled. What to try?
Renewal comes in its own natural rhythm.
You can't grab like a clumsy treasure hunter.
The flash of color escapes in the underbrush.

San Pablo Bay was an inland sea in the Cretaceous.
On its ancient shoreline, a creature among cycads
and sequoia runs, leaps, grasping at dragonflies
that hover near the edge of shallow lagoons,

its brilliant feathers, more extravagant than its relatives,
iridescent in the rays of sun across water.
Fluttering on clumsy undeveloped wings, it finds itself
magically suspended for a moment mid-air,
long enough to pull a meal from the wind.

Poem for My Grandmother "Cassie Hare"

Grandma Hare, I discovered the first big lie in our family,
your untold story, like a brick at my door.
You followed repudiation of the past with flight
from West Bay, Ojibway, First Nation blues.

Left the Island of Manitoulin, sent across
Lake Huron, Naadoweg Gichigami, to school
on the mainland of Ontario. It was 1904,
you had reached your fourteenth year.

Before long, married to a Scotch-Irish son
of a father who owned a big, red brick house, you defied
village women and bobbed your hair (none of *them* dared).
You were seen going to Methodist Church in a motorcar.

I was the child who grew up haunted by the lie,
who awoke with cries, from a dream where I returned
in a storm, crossing rough water on Norisle ferry,
was swept overboard, swam to safety through the rain.

In Grandma Cassie's house, I draw and color pictures—
Indians in war bonnets on ponies. Sometimes I nurse a hurt,
wondering why my blond, blue-eyed cousin is preferred
over a dark-haired, brown-eyed boy like me with an Indian nose.

In her garden, densely hedged with trees, Grandma Hare
chatters and giggles with the youngsters who play
while she weeds her tomatoes. Our game is being Indians,
camped out in "wigwams" made of tree branches.

The former Mohawk Nation became subdivided wheat fields,
towns with British names, Oxford County. A life on lush farms,
King Harvest's bounty, put her children through school.
We grew up with the privileges Grandma bestowed with her lie.

Message on the Water

A cold wind rises
from the San Joaquin River.
Fragile blossoms shudder
in the late winter blast.

Tender petals torn
from branches,
now speckle
the clear mountain stream.

Pink flowers bleed
in cherry colored patterns
that fade, float,
transparent on the water.

They paint their message
on the surface of my thoughts,
as it washes away
in the current, leaving

a remnant—
a memory,
the song they sang
to the shivering wind.

Descansos

"Tucson, Arizona. Great town," I say. She drops
a mixed up cargo of memories on my toes,
epic night-drives through "scary Indian reservations":
Tohono O'odham, Navajo, Pascua Yaqui. Young people
laid in graves somewhere in the desert. Markers
placed close— by a ditch where the car skidded, spun,
rolled, hit a pole, where the flower of Indian youth
flared like a Roman candle, flamed out, guttered,
like California Wonder kids, who also die in reckless cars.

Two cast off pieces of wood, painted white, one nail
makes a cross, with garlands, tinsel, notes pinned,
a sign—"We love you," (a name), Mason jars
of plastic flowers, graced by lit candles
in early weeks, then wayward trash clusters
at the foot of the rickety cross, wind-whipped
monument to mark the place where
something momentous passed—Mother's dream,
a younger brother or sister's inspiration.
Descansos they call them in the Mexican tongue.

So much desperation, "boredom and alcohol," she says.
Self-loathing roams the star-scaped desert. I hear
screech of Rez cars laying scratch on moonless
highways lined with hubcaps, junkers,
ragged rubber curled like corpses of black dogs.
Set farther off the road, distant glimmer of hogans.
"Squalid shacks," she calls them. I think
of the campfires next to abandoned heaps
where some have to shelter, bedding down on car seats.
Now she finds a romantic finish; a benediction
to conclude her sermon… "If these people had Jesus…"
Oh, I don't doubt he helps some, maybe many.
Sweat lodges, vision fasts, talk circles for others. I pray
they awaken to Indian power, the Wakan in themselves.

Let's get out of this night. Leave her bitter Dixie Cup
back there on the asphalt by roadside descansos.
Put a zinnia in the Styrofoam, some Crystal Geyser,
a sign on the road to somewhere. We'll follow
a whiff of tire smoke in the dark, spiral of stars
flung back like a curtain, an unrolled map.

A black shape etched in light
out of corralled dark
out of parched land
comes answering our prayers,
a drinking gourd of cool water.

S. Solomon

Travel Stories

Perhaps what happens after sixty is not
a beginning of anything; not like a divorce.
It is just as likely to be seasonal, au naturel,
waking to a half-remembered
dream in search of direction.

On a clear day the Sierra can be seen from Mt. Diablo,
but when you are eight years old and the year is 1950,
the Sierra is a direction of nearly seven hours, a slow
movement of time to be endured until Echo Summit. Then
with Tahoe in view, even an eight year old can grasp the thrill
of descent, every cell of her being stores it away.

The trick is not to tell anyone the stories you make up.
The traveler must not fall asleep, for once the eyes close
the Indian lovers who leap to their deaths are hidden,
as is the cannon in its little house, set back
from the American River, on a hillside of dense pine.
Mostly you escape the confines of the wood-paneled station wagon.
You are with the wagon train on its way to Placerville or even better,
atop a sure-footed horse with U.S. Mail bags destined for Twin Bridges.

Perhaps what happens after sixty is another story. It may be
immobility has its own direction, a location of silence more seductive
than the thrill of any descent. It may also be the same story.

A Note of Thanksgiving

Inside the word
is a world not kind
to thanksgiving

where no thing is
returned whole
beyond color and

counting consists
of a cleverness
invented by naming

nothing uncalled for
or acquired in haste.

Chairs, tables, beds,
all easily confused
in their similarity

to the faces
of children
misplaced

or misnamed
in the absence
of order.

Only the goldfish
mirrored large
remain familiar.

Swimming Instructions
For Elaine

You are born onto the wide
field of your mother's skin,
shine pure like her mother's voice,
Maidele, this is how you will learn to swim,
from one woman's voice to another's.

Pay no attention to the fathers.
The papas are asleep in their beards.

You will learn to swim. Your aunts
will give you lessons, books about
breathing for long periods,
inhaling for years at a time.
They will tell you to swim with your eyes open.

Pay no attention to the uncles.
They sleep in the arms of their brothers.

Swimming is nothing like walking.
Under water you move in large
slow strokes, deep breaths.
It is like nothing else you need to know.
It is nothing less than
knowing how not to drown.

Do not heed your brothers.
They dream the sleep of their fathers.

The day will come like water.
You will be called upon to leap into it.
You will bring your books,
your needles and threads,
your bubba's voice and the voice of her mother.

Your eyes will remain open.
You will swim across your mother's field,
Your feet will not touch the ground,
the sky will be in your grasp.

You will swim past the men
who have fallen asleep.

In the morning your mother
will tell your story.
She will tell the men
that you have gone,
that you did not drown.

Walking The Dog At Lake Tahoe In The Snow

Trees make no sound
and a cloud-crowded sky
is mute in your absence.

New snow
carries itself
to lake's edge.

Children come with
summer pails,
pack snow into ice forts,
abandon themselves
to this huge season.

The dog cannot
believe her luck.
She is into the drifts,
drunk and without scent.

Fleas have no defense
against this cold.
It is a murderous landscape
in which the voice once uttered
is taken up and hushed.

In this new January,
even if you'd lived,
I would hear nothing.

The Untying

He loosens himself from father
into something more and less,
a strange phenomenon
in which family dinners
become rituals of change.

He tells stories of young men
who wrote for the movies
before movies spoke,
of his photographer uncle
and a distant cousin
who played the Orpheum
on the vaudeville circuit.

He tells stories from behind
a face we hardly know,
each tale a preface for the next,
until the table is crowded with
great grandparents, college professors,
an old pit bull, an assortment
of uncles and neighbors and Nora Bayes,
who once had her music arranged
by George Gershwin himself.

But this is a new story,
it is of his heart and
in its newness,
nothing is so fantastic
as the approach of his death,
the re-spelling of his name
coming apart, letter by letter.
The letting go, story by story.

Empty Room
For my daughter

For rent,
for want
of space
for the heart.

Flower gone,
garden emptied
of root room
in rented heart.

Flower space,
soil, water,
gone for want
of rooted heart.

Root pulled out,
blood soil spent,
the misplanted
miscarried
away.

A Tale Told At The American River

The mountain gives birth to night,
to all nights recorded and ordered.

We climb into sleep,
careful to replace stones
and scrub brush with words
spoken in green tones,
a mountain tongue.

At river's edge
I hear your breath
heavy with fish eggs and tadpoles,
the life of your chest.

This is the story you tell:

"A maintenance worker fell five stories headfirst down an
elevator shaft, and was amazed that he was still alive when he
hit ground." *S.F. Chronicle*

Let's begin at the end like daylight, let go of the man,
a star shoved off the celestial map and
compare his life to the minnow, unrestricted and
down-stream with no thought of rock or story.

Why the workman happened to be on the fifth floor of a particular
building is not known. The fact is he turned, thinking of what he
had meant to bring but had left behind, and stepped back into the
elevator. This story tells us that retrieval may be fraught with
unthinkable danger.

It is not known what his wife said to him after being called to the
scene. Whatever she promised while at his hospital bed is also not
part of the story. But we do know his children, at the dinner table that
night, with his chair empty, ate everything on their plates.

The man knew his screams, following close behind his flailing arms, would not save him. He was a man who knew how things worked and knew a scream to be useless in the mouth of a fool. The maintenance worker was no fool. He wove his fear into cables and broke his fall before reaching the bottom of the elevator shaft.

A story of amazement is best
told outdoors and at its end
we close our eyes,
let the fire dwindle,
listen to the multiple sound
we call river.

Paradise

Stand still.

Look at the hand held
out in front of you,
not a hand, an apple.

Stand like a tree.
Look at your branches,
bend to the hand.

This is how
I will embrace
what is offered.

Whatever words I speak are
what you hear, like apple,
roundredround, eaten by the ear.

Listen.

Hear the juice
tartsweet
on your tongue.

Seeing Clearly

It is the long day,
midnoon begun at dawn
with smoke rising,
the fabric of a jealous lover,
demanding it all back,
a reckoning of old growth
and the haunting
of snow fallen into a
misery of insufficiency.
It is too late for talk.
There will be no kissing.
The longing for green
is already aflame and
the wind that winds its way
from canyon to canyon,
in and out of scrub brush
is beyond redemption.
Heat goes mad with desire,
licks straight up aspen and pine.
Wildfire speaks a scorched
and acrid tongue.
When night falls
it too will fail
to bring this
to an end,
for embers,
like passion,
remember and
have a patience
all their own.

Out of Baltimore

Read in The Baltimore Sun, March 2001

Comes news of an ocean's birth and
I am reminded that nothing
known goes uncharted.

Children spill out like so many
notions whose time has come.
The keeping tabs has begun.

I trace them back to passion,
its slow colors quickening
into our own mythology and
not unlike Dr. Frank's comets,
those carbon-covered snowballs race
at breakneck speeds, hurl themselves
hell-bent on penetration,
on breaking through atmospheric walls
and like ourselves, surrender
to the heat, the power to alter
one mass for another.

Dr. Louis A. Frank has uncovered
the ultraviolet truth:
not even Nature
can resist Herself.

Thestoryteller

I have thought up four children,
a dog, a cat and fleas that bite.
I did not make up the fleas.
The fleas are real. I know they are
real because they bite.

I cannot unthink the four children.
They return like an echo; dismembered
words in search of their origin,
so I make beds and have them
lie down. I tell them stories
to carry into night.

> *The first story is a boy*
> *in white cutting wood.*
> *He is in a field flat as day,*
> *there is no wind but his sigh,*
> *rasp of his saw. Before this field*
> *there was a forest and beyond*
> *the limit of field wait the boy's parents,*
> *their bodies lean on rusted axes,*
> *beyond them wait the planters and sowers.*
> *This is a story of patience.*

> *The second story is of a child*
> *at a table waiting for supper.*
> *Across the table on the wall*
> *a blackboard with riddles hangs*
> *aslant. The parents write riddles*
> *in their native tongue and*
> *for each right answer a morsel*
> *is won. The parents are proud*
> *their child is clever and fat.*
> *This is a story of hunger.*

The third story is a man alone.
He is neither here nor there, but
inside his loneness. For a long while
he does nothing. Then he thinks
to name each part of his body.
He gives names to all he can touch and
when names are exhausted he calls them
by numbers, then by letters, then
by letters with numbers.
This is a story of possibility.

The fourth story is of a woman
who nurses the world with only
one breast. It is a magic breast
kept in a box beneath her bed.
The box is her salvation and to each
child born the breast is offered and
like magic she begins to grow
large into her own death.
This is a story of tyranny.

I put the stories in suitcases,
each numbered according to name.
On top of each story I put in
a dog, a cat and fleas that bite.
I wrap the children's fingers
around the handles and tell them they
must not let go. I tell them
this is your story, you must
carry it always.

Marc Hofstadter

Buddy, My Dog for a Week

I – *During the Week*

I lie curled in bed, knees to belly,
like you, Buddy.
I flop down on chairs.
Yawning, I bare incisors.
I gulp down big chunks of beef
with sauce.
Every once in a while
I sigh without warning.
I'm trying to be like you
because then you'll stay with me forever—
each breath I take,
each heartbeat matching yours.

II – *After the Week*

You taught me how to sniff the breeze
for pine sap and rank moss,
gape at the mad rush of a squirrel up a trunk,
hear goldfinches click branches
with tin feet,
thrill to winter sun turning the sky
blue with joy,
relish beef as though it were
my last meal,
love with tongue and eye,
be in the world and of the world,
and then you taught me to let go.

Was mir die Liebe erzählt
for David

What love tells me
is that some things go deeper than thought.
Quince blossoms, your lips on my cheek,
a line of song flowing on and on . . .
What can I wish for except what is,
since it includes your nose, your mild gaze?
I want to be like a melody that lingers
regardless of beginnings and ends.
I want to be like Mahler, who triumphed,
died young, left me this theme.

Gustav Mahler called the last movement of his Third Symphony
"What Love Tells Me".

The Return
for David

Things are looking up.
Our ducks are back.
Who would have thought it:
a whole year and no sign—
flown to Brazil, Belize?—
but here they are,
green-headed mallard
and his speckled brown wife
looking up at our screen door again,
quacking. We toss out
cracked corn, which they snap up
with leathery bills.
Later we catch them peering
in from the atrium
with velvet brown eyes
like yours.
Will they stay now?
Do they love us?

Rainbow

I picked it apart with my prism,
separating red from orange,
orange from yellow,
yellow from gold,
each color distinct
from the others,
individual, pure.
I thought of myself
as an adventurer of color.
Then I napped, and in my dream
red people cried because
they'd never known an orange person,
orange people wanted to be yellow,
yellow people were stuck forever
in yellowness. I awoke
and looked out the window
wishing to see the old,
multicolored myth,
the one with a pot at its end,
but there was only blue sky.

A Little Night Music
for Arnold Schoenberg

Winter rain beats time to your
piano concerto with jagged leaps and runs
and my heart keeps pace with the jumpy rhythms
of the night and all its moony fantasies
as my pen jots fragments of jazz notes
surging from zigzag movements of the dark,
turns toward dawn and I drowse,
my head abuzz with little strums and squeaks,
eeriness made close and comforting
by your hero's hand.

Empty Places

The back alleys of movie theaters,
haunted by dumpsters and corpses of trash;
long highways in the country so remote
no car or truck's in sight;
parking lots at dawn
deserted but for an attendant up all night;
the vast wheat fields of Iowa seen from a jet
with no sign of man or house at all;
and the vacant homes of Hopper,
baring vulnerable walls
to the cruelties of the sunset:
these places I love,
for I see in them
my own emptiness.

Son House

You toiled out onto the stage,
guitar in one hand, white handkerchief
in the other. You said, "I'se jes' an ole
man, and I cain't play the geetar like
I use' to, but I'se gonna try."
You drew out steel-gray notes
that rose and flew off like
mourning doves into the clouds.
You'd pulled your feet from the mud
of Mississippi to come up
to our white-bread campus and teach
us something we couldn't learn in class.
Now you're in those clouds,
and I'm here trying to emulate your voice.
I'm just an old man, and I can't sing
like I used to, but I'se gonna try.

New York City Trash-Talk

I drew bus exhaust into my lungs
with pleasure, thinking it more real
than anything else I knew,
loved the garbage strewn
in Broadway gutters mixed
with smutty snow and ice
to congeal into pungent pudding.
I gazed delighted at the starlings,
black, aggressive millions, who'd mass
above the West Side Highway
at dusk, dirtying the sky
with their thick bodies.
And the rough, brown-skinned boys,
pants tight, shirts ripped,
who'd pass me on 96th Street,
eyes bold and dangerous,
arms swinging like the wind
threatening to throw into my face
thrilling bits of trash:
chewed gum,
tobacco butts,
spit from wet, dark mouths.

Blaze

I grasped their manes, stroked their soft necks,
whispered endearments into their nervous ears:
no horse could resist me.
Child though I was, I tamed the pinto
no one else could ride, marched it proudly
down the festooned street of my home town
in the Fourth of July parade.
In summer camp I adopted Zorro,
black gelding whose quick, bumpy
gallop pleased me. One day a counselor
who disliked me put me on Blaze,
gray, dappled filly, whose long, loping
strides threw me. I rolled over to avoid
being trampled by the horse behind,
dusted off my chinos, walked the mile
back to camp, never mounted
one of my beloveds again.

Breeze in the Branches

Don't ask for more than a breeze in the branches.
Don't expect the sun to imprint a brassy crown
on your naked skull, the midnight moon
to last all morning, the oriole
to perch on your finger for human food.
Light blooms until its petals collapse to the soil.
So, your heart.
Try to imprison stars in a cage,
the sea in a stone,
you'll fail.
Release the creature
trapped in your clenched fist.
Let it go.

You

Oh utter word that roots at the heart of the world,
let me see! I'm a worm rodent beast
who gazes up at your indistinguishable face
with all the ecstasy of humiliating death
I'm your servant child brother who obeys your commands
here in beds bookstores offices You screw me
like an overpowering ardent lover I submit
I've known you forever and don't know you at all
You set the great cymbals crashing the lightning
forking that illuminates the narrow path
through vines fronds savage blossoms
and the cities littered with rubbish and bodies
You don't explain You gaze with burning eyes
over the desert of my fate You live in
Blake St. John of the Cross Rimbaud you charge
electric tongues with the death roar of your infinite mercy
Drug visions seizures shudders are the convulsions
of your breast upon which men like me founder
Ultimate orgasm of the seas throw me foaming at the mouth
and ejaculating into the spume Rock me in your
nursing arms Show me how to thread my way
infinitesimal frightened unsure into this endless roar
Oh ultimate, I name you God Tao Spirit
I don't know what to call you You have
been with me from the beginning I am with you
beyond all ends Carry me into the valley
Hold me in the calm lake of your dream
Make me whole with your fierce grip

Acknowledgments

ৎ৯৩৵

An earlier version of Joseph Chaiklin's "Autumn Squirrels" appeared in the *Connecticut Writer*.

Marc Hofstadter's poems "Buddy, My Dog for a Week," "The Return," "Empty Places," "Son House," "New York City Trash-Talk," "Blaze," "Breeze in the Branches," and "You" appeared previously in his book *Luck* (Scarlet Tanager Books, Oakland, CA, 2008). Also, "The Return" appeared in the magazine *PKA's Advocate* and "Son House" in *Cape Rock*.

Florence Miller's poem, "Raven Reads the Fog," appeared previously in *Blue Unicorn*; "Salvage," in *Journal of New Jersey Poets*; "Death in Carvoeiro," in *Senior Moments*; "Forced Landing," in slightly different form in *Poems by Shakespeare's Sisters* (Shakespeare's Sisters Press); and haiku from "Still," appeared in *Eleven Renga*, and *Yes* (Jade Mountain Press).

Elaine Starkman's "31 Flavors Invade Japan/French Vanilla," appeared in *Cæsura*, Origins Issue, San José Poetry Center, Spring 2008; her poem, "Northern California Freeway, 8:30 A.M.," appeared in *Oracle*, Brewton-Parker College, Vol. 6, 2007, under the title "Hitchhiker."

About the Authors

❧⦿❧

Joseph Chaiklin was born in Connecticut, attended the University of Connecticut where he received a B.A. in English literature and Speech and Theatre Arts, edited the campus literary magazine and was a prize winner for poetry in the University's annual writing competition. He earned an M.A. in Speech Pathology at Ohio State University and a Ph.D. in Audiology at Stanford University. During his career as an educator, clinical audiologist and researcher, he published many research articles in scientific journals, co-edited two editions of *Hearing Measurement: A Book of Readings,* and was Associate Editor of *The Journal of Speech and Hearing Research.* Email: jchaiklin@astound.net

Marc Hofstadter was born in New York City and earned his doctorate in literature from the University of California at Santa Cruz. He has taught American literature at U.C. Santa Cruz, the Université d'Orléans (on a Fulbright), and Tel Aviv University, and for twenty-five years served as the librarian of the San Francisco Municipal Railway. His poems, translations and essays have appeared in over sixty magazines, and he has published four books of poetry: *House of Peace, Visions, Shark's Tooth,* and *Luck.* He lives in Walnut Creek, California with his partner David Zurlin. Email: mhofstad@ifn.net

Dave Holt was born in Toronto, Ontario, Canada, of Irish, English, and Ojibway (Chippewa) Indian ancestry. He began as a songwriter, a vocation that led to his move to California in 1970. He entered San Francisco State Creative Writing program (B.A. '93, and M.A. '95), and has published poetry in journals and magazines. He was a prizewinner in the Thomas Merton Foundation's Poetry of the Sacred. In 2005, he founded a Native Peoples Team Members Group for American Indian employees at Wells Fargo Bank. Email: bohohwymus@aol.com

Florence Miller taught creative writing at McClymonds High School in Oakland, California, where she advised the award winning literary magazine, *Flamingo*. The film *Can You Hear Me*, based on her students' poetry, aired on PBS. A founding member of the collective, Shakespeare's Sisters, she co-edited *Crazy Ladies* and *Poems by Shakespeare's Sisters* as well as the peace anthologies *Dreaming of Wings and State of Peace: The Women Speak*. Miller co-authored *Eleven Renga, Yes*, and *A String of Monarchs* with Alexis Rotella. Email: flopoems@gmail.com

S. Solomon is a third generation East Bay Californian. She was a bookseller for seven years at the late Bonanza Books and is currently employed as Bookseller Emeritus at the lively and thriving independent, Clayton Books. Her poetry and prose has been published in local and national literary magazines and journals. She currently writes a book review column for The Clayton Pioneer and holds an MA in English/Creative Writing from SFSU. Email: memorie3@yahoo.com

Elaine Starkman currently teaches at Osher Life Long Learning Institute, Cal State Extension and in Contra Costa adult schools. She is the author *of Learning to Sit in the Silence: A Journal of Caretaking* and co-editor of *Here I Am: Contemporary Jewish Stories from Around the World,* which won the PEN/Oakland Award. Her work has appeared in eclectic journals and on-line. She has won prizes from the Benicia Love Poem Contest, and from Napa College and The Asheville Writers Workshop in prose. Email: Elaine.Starkman@gmail.com.

Breinigsville, PA USA
17 August 2009
222443BV00002B/2/P

9 781598 589658